AN ILLUSTRATED BIOGRAPHY OF JOE DELANEY

HEROIC HEART

THE LEGACY OF A PROFESSIONAL FOOTBALL PLAYER

By **Frank Murphy**
and **Charnaie Gordon**

Art by **Anastasia**
Magloire Williams

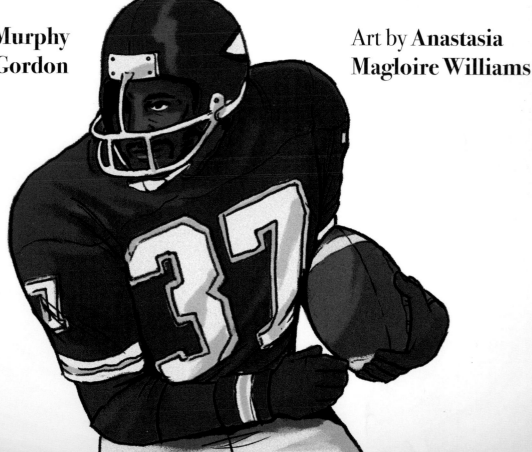

Printed in China ISBN: 978-1-63727-316-6

His youth.

October 30, 1958.
JoAnn and Joe Delaney were born.
Twins!
But tiny Joe almost didn't get to take
his

first

breath

Joe was born with a "veil" over his face.
A rare condition at birth.
It was removed.
And Joe swallowed
his first small pant of air.
Some believe any baby born with this veil is...
one day
destined to die of
drowning.
In many cultures it is believed
that being born with this veil means
a baby is destined for
greatness.

Joe was the third
of eight children.
Three boys and
five girls all living
under one roof
with two parents
in a small town called
Henderson, Texas.

WELCOME TO
HAUGHTON

1967.
Joe and his family
started a new life
in a new place
in an old wooden house
in a town with fewer
than a thousand people.
His hometown.
Haughton, Louisiana.

His passion.

His first love was running.

Then running with a football.

Joe was small,

but he sure was mighty,

especially on the football field.

In seventh grade Joe declared,

"Momma, I'm gonna be a pro football player.

I'm gonna make you proud of me one day."

Joe's father was a truck driver.

He worked long hours and longer days.

He believed playing football was

nonsense and wouldn't allow it.

But Joe's siblings teamed up and finished all of Joe's daily chores,

so he could secretly chase his dream.

Haughton High School
was the place where Joe
became an all-state star player on his team.

Joe loved running.
As a boy, he would run by one house
more than the others.

There was a girl Joe had his eyes on.
He only had eyes for her. Forever.
His childhood sweetheart, Carolyn.

In college, Joe and
Carolyn married.

They started a family.
Three girls.
Tamika, Crystal, Joanna.
Now Joe had something he loved,
even more than running and football.
His own family.

Joe's speed.

Some of the biggest and best colleges
wanted Joe to come run track and play football.
But Joe stayed loyal to his hometown state.
He chose little Northwestern State University.

June 6, 1981,
The NCAA college track and field
championship.
Joe's team included
Victor Oatis,
Mario Johnson,
Mark Duper,
and Joe.
Small town runners running against
BIG time runners:
A future Olympic gold medalist,
A Heisman Trophy winner,
and one of the world's fastest men.

But...together,
with great desire in their hearts...
Joe and his teammates ran like

lightning

and in 39 seconds
they won the NCAA
4 by 100 meter relay.

And on the college football field
no one caught Joe.

He became an All-American.

One of the best running backs
in the country.

His grit.
His whole life people told Joe
"You're too small."
Through high school.
Then college.
Joe proved he belonged.
But the NFL had the best and biggest football players.
Would Joe be
big enough?
Tough enough?

The Kansas City Chiefs chose Joe.
They knew Joe ran like lightning,
but some still doubted his size.
Joe showed up early to practice
and he stayed late, each day.

Always lifting others with a handshake
or a high-five.

Joe's heart was dedicated to being
the best teammate
and football player he could be.

His relentless heart.
October 4th, 1981,
Joe came off the bench

and *ran*,

ran for 101 yards and a touchdown!
The next week Joe ran for
106 yards.
And he had 104 yards receiving!
Joe showed his team, the NFL, and the world
he was tough enough.

In one game,
Joe ran for 193 yards and a touchdown.
All while playing with

cracked
ribs,

a broken
wrist,

a sprained
knee.

Joe's relentless heart didn't
allow him to complain.
Not once.

Joe started in the NFL's all-star game –
the Pro Bowl.
He won the Rookie of the Year Award –
the best of all
the newest players in the NFL.
His teammates voted Joe
the Chiefs' Most Valuable Player.

GO CHIEFS!

GAME DAY

JOE DELANEY

JOE DEL

37

37

After seven long years of losing
the Chiefs finished with a
winning record.
Joe's relentless heart pumped

life

into the hopes of his team and
their fans.

His generous heart.

Joe made thousands of dollars.
But he always gave his paycheck
to his wife for their
family.
All he wanted was a few dollars
for a soda pop at the corner store.

Joe was famous, now.
But that didn't stop him from
mowing his neighbor's lawn, each week,
when no one else would.
Or taking neighborhood boys
to the barbershop,
when no one else would.
Or buying his high school football
team uniforms and more,
when no one else would.
Or paying for the funeral
of a former teacher,
when no one else could.

His heroic heart.

June 29th, 1983.
Summer sun sweltering.
Thousands at a kids' festival.
Barbecues. Dancing. Laughing.
Softball and summer fun.
Three boys splashing in a pond.

Suddenly, screaming and shouting.
The boys sunk under and didn't come up.
Without hesitating.
Without thinking of himself.
Joe **rushed** to the water, running,
when no one else would.

And it didn't matter that

Joe couldn't swim well.

Joe jumped in...

One boy...
...made it out.
Shouting and screaming.
Joe went under the water.

Again.

Frantic seconds turned into eternal minutes...

Joe...

did not

come up

from

the

water . . .

Later that day
Joe's family heard the news.

Hearts
sunken

and

shattered.

Then, the world
heard the news...

Joe's legacy

Five days later. July 4th.
Summer sun...sweltering, again.
3,000 people
crowded in Haughton High School's gymnasium
—the only place big enough to hold
so many people.
Vice President George H.W. Bush delivered
President Ronald Reagan's words.

"He made the ultimate sacrifice
by placing the lives of three children
above regard
for his own safety.
By the supreme example of
courage and compassion,
this brilliantly gifted young man
left a spiritual legacy
for his fellow Americans."

Tears. Crying. Memories.
Memories of Joe Delaney,
who was destined...
...for greatness.
...for love.
...for kindness.
...and for sacrifice.

His heroic heart.

Joe's heroic heart lives on

...in his three daughters
who all made careers in service to others.
In his wife, Carolyn, and his family,
who created a foundation
dedicated to teaching children
leadership skills and
water safety.

Joe Delaney's story is not meant
to be put on a pedestal and admired.
It is meant to work in our world.
The true legacy of Joe's story
rests inside of YOU and what you choose to do

with your own heroic heart.

Joe Delaney

DID YOU KNOW?

- Although Joe's jersey number 37 is not officially retired by the Chiefs, no player has ever worn it since.

- Joe may be the all-time fastest player who ever played in the NFL. In high school, Joe ran the 100 yard dash in 9.4 seconds. He holds the Northwestern State University 200 meter dash record with a time of 20.64 seconds.

- Joe Delaney's name is in the Chiefs Ring of Honor and he was inducted into the College Football Hall of Fame and the Louisiana Sports Hall of Fame.

- In 2021, a two-mile stretch of I-435 that goes past Arrowhead Stadium in Kansas City was renamed the "Joe Delaney Memorial Highway."

- On October 28, 1978, while playing in college for Northwestern State against Nicholls State University, Joe carried the ball 28 times and gained 299 yards; 263 of the yards came in the second half. This is still an NCAA record. He also scored four touchdowns in that game—one for 90 yards!

- The only thing that Joe ever bought for himself was a car; it was his only prized possession—a baby blue 1981 Mercury Cougar.

- Joe is the uncle of Carolina Panthers wide receiver Terrace Marshall Jr.

Family photos provided by Joanna Delaney.

A Legacy Lives On

When Joe Delaney sacrificed his life, it was one week before the start of training camp for his third season with the Chiefs—he was only 24 years old. On that day, June 20th, 1983, Marvin Dearman was the diver who tried to save Joe and the other two boys. Decades later Mr. Dearman lobbied to have a permanent memorial to honor Joe at the park where it happened. Today, at Chennault Park in Monroe, Louisiana, there is a memorial to Joe, honoring his heroic act. There is also a park named for Joe in his hometown of Haughton, Louisiana.

Carolyn Delaney and Joe's family started a foundation, the Delaney 37 Foundation, to help children and young adults learn financial literacy, leadership skills, and provide swimming instruction for kids. For more information visit: www.delaney37foundation.com.

The Government Employees Health Association, Inc. (G.E.H.A.), the Hunt Family Foundation, and the YMCA of Greater Kansas City have teamed up to support the need for addressing barriers to health equity through the Joe Delaney Learn to Swim Program. Each year, hundreds of kids are learning to swim - commemorating and preserving the memory, deeds, and legacy of Joe Delaney.

All three of Joe's and Carolyn's daughters pursued careers in health and medical service. Tamika, the oldest, became a dialysis technician. Crystal became a registered nurse and lab technician. And Joanna, who was just three months old when Joe died, became a medical coder. Joanna is proud that she and her sisters dedicated their lives to helping others. "We saw he had a genuine heart and a heart that cared for people, so we all kind of have his heart."

Did you know several studies conducted over the years consistently indicate that over 50% of Black Americans don't know how to swim?

A recent national study conducted at YMCAs by the USA Swimming Foundation and the University of Memphis, concluded that 64 percent of Black children cannot swim. Compare that number to 40 percent of white children that don't know how to swim.

The fatal-drowning rate of Black children in America is three times higher than white children. How staggering is that?

I've always known swimming was an important life skill. However, I didn't learn to swim until I was an adult in my forties. When Frank Murphy told me the inspirational story of Joe Delaney I decided to fully commit to learning how to swim. FINALLY. Thanks, Frank!

Growing up, our family didn't live in an area where we had access to pools. I have fond memories of visiting our local beach one or two times during the summer in my childhood years. However, the ocean was not an ideal place for me to learn how to swim.

My older sister and I took adult swimming lessons years ago at our local YMCA, but I failed miserably. Not only was I scared of drowning, I also didn't want to get my hair wet. Back then, my hair was chemically straightened (relaxed) with a perm. And since pool water can be detrimental to Black hair, getting it wet in the pool was something I always tried to avoid at all costs.

Having chlorine or salt in the water can work against chemically relaxed hair or Black hair in its natural state. If your hair isn't cared for properly, you can end up having breakage or hair shedding. When Black, afro-textured hair is in its natural state, (without being chemically relaxed) it shrinks up when it gets wet. Hair shrinkage can cause embarrassment and shame for some Black women and young girls.

Black women have a complex relationship with hair that often stems from trying to live up to Eurocentric beauty standards.

This includes believing the idea that only certain hair textures, body types, and facial features are often seen as "more attractive" than others. I know these things took a toll on my mental health, self-esteem, and overall perception of myself when I was growing up. Those ideals stuck with me well into my twenties. That was before I learned to fully love and accept myself just the way I was in my natural state, including loving my natural hair.

Lastly, Black people have a complicated history and relationship with water in general.

From enslaved people drowning in the water during their voyage from Africa to America, being hosed down with water from fire hydrants during the Civil Rights era, being chased from and attacked in local public pools due to segregation, to feeling shame or being ridiculed when our natural hair shrinks up when it gets wet.

Over the years, I have learned and unlearned many things I used to believe like "Black people don't swim." Today I'm proud to say, "Yes, Black people do swim." And I am one of those people all thanks to Mr. Joe Delaney.

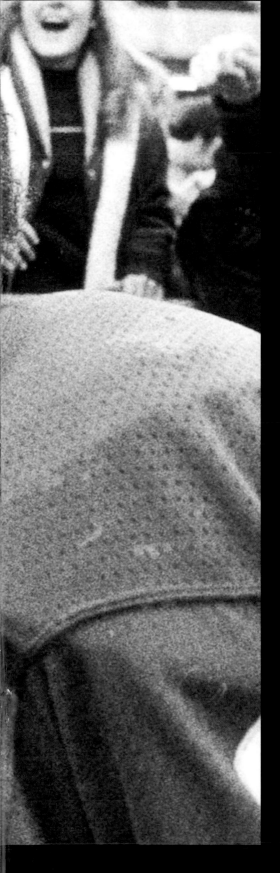

Left photo: Peter Read Miller via AP
Center photo: Dan Peak/*The Kansas City Star*/TNS; Newscom
Right photo: Focus on Sport/Getty Images

ABOUT THE AUTHORS

Frank Murphy has been teaching elementary school for over 30 years and writing children's books for over 20 years. He is the author of books for children including A Boy Like You, A Girl Like You, A Friend Like You, and Fearless Heart, in addition to many historical biographies for early readers. He lives near Philadelphia with his family. Sharing Joe Delaney's story as a picture book has been a long time passion project for Frank.

AUTHOR'S NOTE: *It was the summer between my junior and senior years of high school when I found out about Joe Delaney and his heroic act on June 29th, 1983. I had collected his football cards and marveled at his electric highlights on TV. His story has stayed with me all these years. After becoming a children's book writer, I began to craft his story into a picture book text - this was in the late 2000s. The more I read about Joe, the more I learned that he led with his heart his whole life. I tried to get Joe's story published, but was unsuccessful. After writing and having* Fearless Heart *published, I was inspired again to share Joe's story with the world. But this time I decided to write his story in free verse (like* Fearless Heart*) and invite my friend and two-time co-author Charnaie Gordon to collaborate with me. The way Joe's story connects with Charnaie and Anastasia is just another example of how Joe's story is still impacting our world today. Over my 30-plus years of teaching elementary school I've frequently taught students about Joe and the story of his life. Now, having this picture book as a resource for teaching and for the world to read means a lot.*

Charnaie Gordon is a Diversity and Inclusion Advocate, podcast host, and Digital Creator. She is also the author of the picture books *A Kids Book About Diversity, Lift Every Voice and Change, Etta Extraordinaire,* and many more. Charnaie's blog, Here Wee Read, is where she expresses her creativity and passion for reading, diverse literature, and literacy. She's also the founder of her children's literacy non-profit organization, 50 States 50 Books, Inc., where they collect and donate diverse children's books to deserving kids in each of the 50 U.S. states. She lives in Connecticut with her husband and two children.

Anastasia Magloire Williams is an illustrator and visual storyteller working in children's literature and entertainment media. Her artistic mission is to elevate untold and diverse stories. Illustrating this story struck a particular chord in her—she was once saved from drowning as a child by a hero like Joe Delaney. You can see more of her work at **www.anadraws.com**

ABOUT THE PUBLISHER

Triumph Books is the nation's leading sports book publisher—an independent publisher founded in 1989. In addition to working with some of the most celebrated coaches and athletes in the world, they publish oral and team histories, pictorials, and rule books for every major American sports league. Triumph Books seeks to champion authors and stories that reflect the beautifully diverse and colorful world we share, uplifting readers with stories of perseverance, courage, and incredible strength.